Glowing with Gratitude

Copyright

All rights reserved. Without limiting the rights under copyright reserved above, no part of this publication may be reproduced, stored in or introduced into a retrieval system, or transmitted, in any other form or by any means (electronic, mechanical, photocopying, recording or otherwise), without the permission of both the copyright owner and the publisher of this book. Except in the case of brief quotations embodied in critical reviews and specific other non-commercial uses permitted by copyright law.

Created by: NikkNakk Designs
With immense gratitude to my family and friends who love and support me with my creative adventures.

First published in 2019
© 2019 Westminster Designs Pty Ltd
ISBN 978-1-92542-231-3

Gratitude helps you to grow and expand; gratitude brings joy and laughter into your life and into the lives of all those around you.

Eileen Caddy (1917-2006)
Irish/English author, spiritual teacher and one of the founders of the Findhorn Community

Introduction

My reason for creating Glowing with Gratitude is to share the difference a daily gratitude practice has made in my life and hope it makes a positive difference in your life too.

This journal can be kept for many years capturing moments, which can be treasured with a smile. I find writing in my gratitude journal helps me cultivate a positive and happy mindset, which I call my Gratitude Glow.

Finding gratitude in the world around me has helped me discover joy in small things even when times are tough, I now focus on the good in my life instead of the adverse.

There is always something lovely even on most challenging days, we just have to search deep inside, and it will appear.

Being thankful is something I try to do every day either first thing in the morning to set my intention to have a happy, positive day or at night to give thanks for the great moments and people in my life.

My wish for you completing this book is that you find the inspiration to finish it one page at a time, relishing in the magical moments in your life and thankful they occurred.

I hope the 'memory joggers' encourage you on the days you cannot seem to find anything for which to be grateful and the quotes motivate you to celebrate your daily gratitude practice as a way of life and receive its many benefits which may include;

1. **More loving and quality relationships.**

2. **An improvement in physical health, including sleeping, longer and better.**

3. **Improved self-esteem and confidence.**

4. **People who practice gratitude are more relaxed, calm and happy.**

5. **Reduced anxiety and depression.**

6. **Grateful people exercise more and have more vitality.**

7. **Gratitude increases mental strength and resilience.**

I created this book to help you find your Gratitude Glow.

Today I am grateful for my family
and the special moments we share.

Date   /   /

Today I am grateful for . . .

Date   /   /

Today I am grateful for . . .

Date   /   /

Date   /   /

Today I am grateful for . . .

> "Through the eyes of gratitude,
> everything is a miracle."
> – Mary Davis

Date   /   /

Today I am grateful for the moments
I can spend peacefully alone.

Today I am grateful for . . .

Date   /   /

Today I am grateful for . . .   Date   /   /

Date   /   /

Today I am grateful for . . .

> "Gratitude turns what we have into enough."
> – Anonymous

Date   /   /

Today I am grateful for the love of my parents and their belief in me.

Today I am grateful for . . .   Date   /   /

Today I am grateful for . . .

Date   /   /

Today I am grateful for . . .   Date   /   /

"Giving thanks for abundance is greater than
the abundance itself."
– Rumi

Date   /   /

Today I am grateful for the abundance of nourishing food that supports my body.

Today I am grateful for . . .   Date   /   /

Today I am grateful for . . .

Date   /   /

Today I am grateful for . . .   Date   /   /

> "Gratitude makes sense of our past, brings peace
> for today, and creates a vision for tomorrow."
> – Melody Beattie

Today I am grateful for my partner and our loving relationship.

Date   /   /

Today I am grateful for . . .   Date   /   /

Today I am grateful for . . .

Date   /   /

Today I am grateful for . . .   Date   /   /

> "The essential attributes of a great leader are
> a positive attitude, humility, and gratitude."
> – Debasish Mridha

Today I am grateful for how good I feel when I exercise.

Date   /   /

Today I am grateful for . . .

Date   /   /

Today I am grateful for . . .

Date / /

Date   /   /

Today I am grateful for . . .

> "We often take for granted the very things
> that most deserve our gratitude."
> – Cynthia Ozick

Date   /   /

Today I am grateful for my job and my work colleagues.

Today I am grateful for . . .

Date   /   /

Today I am grateful for . . .   Date   /   /

Date   /   /

Today I am grateful for . . .

....
....
....
....
....
....
....
....
....
....
....
....
....
....
....
....
....
....
....
....

> *"Be mindful. Be grateful. Be positive.*
> *Be true. Be kind."*
> *– Roy T. Bennett*

Date   /   /

Today I am grateful for books I have read and the wisdom I have acquired.

Today I am grateful for . . .

Date   /   /

Today I am grateful for . . .

Date / /

Date   /   /

Today I am grateful for . . .

....
....
....
....
....
....
....
....
....
....
....
....
....
....
....
....
....
....
....
....
....

> *"Nothing is more honourable than a grateful heart."*
> *– Lucius Annaeus Seneca*

Date   /   /

Today I am grateful for my favourite place in nature and how I feel when I am there.

Today I am grateful for . . .   Date   /   /

Today I am grateful for . . .

Date   /   /

Date   /   /

Today I am grateful for . . .

....
....
....
....
....
....
....
....
....
....
....
....
....
....
....
....
....
....
....
....
....
....

> *"Silent gratitude isn't very much use to anyone."*
> *– Gertrude Stein*

Today I am grateful for for my pets and the joy they bring into my life.

Date   /   /

Today I am grateful for . . .

Date   /   /

Today I am grateful for . . .

Date   /   /

Date   /   /

Today I am grateful for . . .

> "The best way to show my gratitude is to accept everything, even my problems, with joy." – *Mother Theresa*

Today I am grateful for my unique body and soul.

Date   /   /

Today I am grateful for . . .   Date   /   /

Date   /   /

Today I am grateful for . . .

Today I am grateful for . . .   Date   /   /

> "Gratitude opens the door to the power, the wisdom, the creativity of the universe. You open the door through gratitude." – Deepak Chopra

Date   /   /

Today I am grateful for my brothers and sisters and the special bond we share.

Today I am grateful for . . .   Date   /   /

Today I am grateful for . . .

Date   /   /

Date   /   /

Today I am grateful for . . .

> "Consider each day to be a white canvas that you can fill with all your love, gratitude and skills to make the day a special, unique and abundant one." – *David John St Clair*

Date   /   /

Today I am grateful for my good night's sleep in my comfortable bed.

Today I am grateful for . . .					Date / /

Today I am grateful for . . .   Date   /   /

Today I am grateful for . . .   Date   /   /

> "Today I choose to live with gratitude for the LOVE that fills my heart, the PEACE that rests within my spirit and the voice of HOPE that says all things are possible." – *Unknown*

Date   /   /

Today I am grateful for my memories of my past and the lessons I have learnt.

Today I am grateful for . . .

Date   /   /

Today I am grateful for . . .   Date   /   /

Date   /   /

Today I am grateful for . . .

"Gratitude is the sign of noble souls."
– Aesop

Date   /   /

Today I am grateful for my smile and how it encourages people to smile back at me.

Today I am grateful for . . .

Date   /   /

Today I am grateful for . . .   Date   /   /

Date   /   /

Today I am grateful for . . .

> "It is only with gratitude that life becomes rich."
> – Deitrich Bonheiffer

Date   /   /

Today I am grateful for the friends in my life
and the moments filled with laughter that we share.

Today I am grateful for . . .

Date   /   /

Today I am grateful for . . .

Date   /   /

Today I am grateful for . . .   Date   /   /

"Gratitude can transform common days into thanksgivings, turn routine jobs into joy, and change ordinary opportunities into blessings." – *William Arthur Ward*

Date   /   /

Today I am grateful for a beautiful piece of art and how it inspires me.

Today I am grateful for . . .   Date   /   /

Today I am grateful for . . .   Date   /   /

Today I am grateful for . . .　　　　　　　　　　Date   /   /

> "As we express our gratitude, we must never forget that the highest appreciation is not to utter words but to live by them." – John F. Kennedy

Date   /   /

Today I am grateful for my home and
the security of somewhere to live.

Today I am grateful for . . .

Date   /   /

Today I am grateful for . . .

Date   /   /

Date   /   /

Today I am grateful for . . .

"The struggle ends when gratitude begins."
— Neil Donald Walsh.

Today I am grateful for my successes in life.

Date   /   /

Today I am grateful for . . .　　　　　　　　Date　 /　 /

Today I am grateful for . . .   Date   /   /

Date   /   /

Today I am grateful for . . .

"Gratitude unlocks the fullness of life."
– *Anonymous*

Date   /   /

Today I am grateful for the beautiful Sunset.

Today I am grateful for . . .

Date   /   /

Today I am grateful for . . .

Date   /   /

Today I am grateful for . . .   Date   /   /

"There is always something to be
grateful for."
– Anonymous

Date   /   /

Today I am grateful for the innovations of technology and how it has improved life for so many people.

Today I am grateful for . . .　　　　　　　　Date　　/　　/

Date   /   /

Today I am grateful for . . .

Today I am grateful for . . .　　　　　　　　　Date　　/　　/

> "Gratitude is one of the most medicinal emotions we can feel. It elevates our moods and fills us with joy."
> – Sara Avant Stover

Today I am grateful for my favourite TV shows.

Date   /   /

Date   /   /

Today I am grateful for . . .

Today I am grateful for . . .   Date   /   /

Date   /   /

Today I am grateful for . . .

....
....
....
....
....
....
....
....
....
....
....
....
....
....
....
....
....
....
....
....
....

> *"The roots of all goodness lie in the soil of appreciation for goodness."*
> – Dalai Lama

Date   /   /

I'm grateful for my successes today and am thankful for the great things that await me tomorrow . . .

Today I am grateful for . . .

Date   /   /

Date   /   /

Today I am grateful for . . .

Today I am grateful for . . .   Date / /

> "Gratitude takes less energy than anger."
> – Kristin Cashore

Date   /   /

Today I am grateful for finding a parking spot when I am in a hurry.

Today I am grateful for . . .   Date   /   /

Today I am grateful for . . .

Date   /   /

Date   /   /

Today I am grateful for . . .

> "Gratitude is when memory is stored in the heart and not in the mind."
> – Lionel Hampton

Today I am grateful for the ability to say No. Date   /   /

Today I am grateful for . . .

Date   /   /

Date   /   /

Today I am grateful for . . .

Date   /   /

Today I am grateful for . . .

> "Let gratitude be the pillow upon which you kneel to say your nightly prayer. And let faith be the bridge you build to overcome evil and welcome good." – *Maya Angelou*

Date   /   /

Today I am grateful for clean water to drink and other necessities I have sometimes taken for granted.

Today I am grateful for . . .   Date   /   /

Today I am grateful for . . .   Date   /   /

Date   /   /

Today I am grateful for . . .

....

....

....

....

....

....

....

....

....

....

....

....

....

....

....

....

....

....

....

....

....

....

....

> *"Joy is the simplest form of gratitude."*
> *– Karl Barth*

Date   /   /

Today I am grateful for my favourite
piece of music and how I feel when I hear it.

Today I am grateful for . . .

Date   /   /

Date   /   /

Today I am grateful for . . .

Date   /   /

Today I am grateful for . . .

> "'Thank you' is the best prayer that anyone could say. I say that one a lot. Thank you expresses extreme gratitude, humility, understanding." – *Alice Walker*

Today I am Grateful for
the Courage to be me.

www.ingramcontent.com/pod-product-compliance
Lightning Source LLC
Chambersburg PA
CBHW071005080526
44587CB00015B/2357